How to Build a Gre[

By John Davidson

Gardening Series

Mendon Cottage Books

JD-Biz Publishing

**Download Free Books!
http://MendonCottageBooks.com**

All Rights Reserved.

No part of this publication may be reproduced in any form or by any means, including scanning, photocopying, or otherwise without prior written permission from JD-Biz Corp Copyright © 2015

All Images Licensed by Fotolia, 123RF, and SDSPlans.

Disclaimer

The information is this book is provided for informational purposes only. The information is believed to be accurate as presented based on research by the author.

The author or publisher is not responsible for the use or safety of any procedure or treatment mentioned in this book. The author or publisher is not responsible for errors or omissions that may exist.

Our books are available at

1. Amazon.com
2. Barnes and Noble
3. Itunes
4. Kobo
5. Smashwords
6. Google Play Books

Download Free Books!
http://MendonCottageBooks.com

Download Greenhouse plans from our website HERE http://sdsplans.com

Table of Contents

Table of Contents 3
Chapter 1 5
Introduction to Greenhouses 5
Design considerations: 5
Choosing a site for your Greenhouse: 6
Chapter 2 8
Types of Greenhouses 8
   Based on Shape: 8
   Based on Utility: 10
   Based on Construction Material: 11
   Based on Covering Materials: 12
Chapter 3 13
Elements of a Greenhouse 13
   Foundations: 13
   Concrete Foundation: 15
   Concrete Slab Foundation: 16
   Wood Foundation: 16
   Plumbing and Wiring: 17
   Flooring: 19
   Advantages of permanent floor: 20
   Advantages of temporary floor: 20
Framing: 20
   Framing of Walls and Roof: 21
   Wall Framing Tips: 22
   Framing of Doors and Vents: 23
   Roof Framing: 24
   Heating: 25
   Calculating Heat Requirements for your Greenhouse: 25
   Heat Conservation Tips: 26
   Cooling: 26
   Evaporative Cooling: 28
Greenhouse Maintenance: 28
Chapter 4 30

Greenhouse Plans 30

Publisher **55**

Chapter 1

Introduction to Greenhouses

A greenhouse is a house made of glass or plastic where plants are grown; it is also called a hothouse or a glasshouse, which allows as much light as possible and protects the plants from winter and cold winds. One can use the greenhouse for the entire planting process i.e., from sowing the seeds to harvesting the produce.

The walls of a greenhouse collect light and convert the accumulated light into heat. The heat thus generated can be moderated and released properly to provide a controlled environment for the plants. The heat released within the greenhouse is absorbed by soil and water, which is retained even after the sun goes down. A greenhouse also helps with the following:

a. It provides protection from the harsh winds that can uproot the plants and/or blow away the seeds.

b. Protects the plants from excess rain, snow, and hailstorm.

c. Helps you to harvest chemical-free produce – you don't have to use chemicals to keep away pests and other insects, as the greenhouse acts as a natural barrier for rodents and pests.

Design considerations:

Before proceeding with constructing a greenhouse, following are some pointers to consider:

1. Decide on the size of the greenhouse – a big greenhouse may sound impressive but maintaining it is difficult; a small greenhouse might turn out to be too small for your plant collection; it is advisable to opt for one size bigger than your planned greenhouse size or to go for expandable greenhouse design.

2. A greenhouse requires time and effort to maintain; even though you can automate the watering and ventilation requirements of the plants, you must still spend time in the greenhouse; calculate the time and effort that you are willing to set aside for the greenhouse.

3. Decide on the budget you are willing to spend on constructing the greenhouse; you can cut corners by using cheap material but using poor quality materials may not retain heat very well and will prove to be expensive in the long run.

Choosing a site for your Greenhouse:

As light is the single most important factor for the greenhouse to work efficiently, you must select a site that receives plenty of sunshine. Plants need a minimum of 6 hours of sunlight. Some of the factors to consider for choosing a site are:

1. The site must be free from shades; it must also be free from shadows cast from buildings, hedges, fences, or any other obstructions.

2. Consider the sun's position throughout the year – your greenhouse might receive maximum sunlight during spring and summer but this will change during winter when the sun changes its position.

3. Sunlight is very important during winter to keep the greenhouse warm; any obstacles casting shadows will stay much longer during winter than any other season.

4. Placing the greenhouse in south or southeast direction of your house will provide maximum exposure to sunlight.

5. You can also try to site your greenhouse in the east direction of your house.

6. If you have limited choices to site your greenhouse, you will have to supplement it with additional lighting and heating sources.

7. The entrance of the greenhouse must be faced away from prevailing winds in order prevent loss of heat.

8. Water and electric outlets must be nearby to the greenhouse; so must be the drains to drain away water.

Chapter 2

Types of Greenhouses

There are many types of greenhouse designs that one can choose from. The types can be broadly classified based on shape, utility, construction materials, and covering materials.

Based on Shape:

a. **Lean-to Greenhouse:** A lean-to greenhouse is attached to the house or garage and therefore has easy access to water, electricity, and also gains heat from the house or garage. It is common to attach a lean-to greenhouse on the south-facing wall of the house. However, such greenhouses must have proper ventilation to avoid overheating; the greenhouse must also be protected from snow sliding from the house roof. A lean-to greenhouse is also restricted in height and the materials used in construction must compliment the materials of the attached structure. A lean-to greenhouse usually has a maximum width of 12feet and is restricted to a couple of benches of plants.

b. **Freestanding Greenhouse:** A freestanding greenhouse, as the name suggests can be located anywhere on your property; the design and materials used for constructing this greenhouse can be different from the main house. Since all the four sides are exposed to the sun, this structure receives maximum sunlight. The drawback to freestanding greenhouse is that it might require a concrete foundation depending on the size of the structure; necessary arrangements must be made for water, electricity, and ventilation, thereby adding to the cost of construction.

c. **Quonset Greenhouse:** This greenhouse also called a hoop house has an arched roof, which allows efficient transfer of load to the ground; this is not only economical but also well suited for domestic purposes. The hoop is usually made of PVC pipe and is installed at every 4 feet. The covering used is made of construction grade polythene, which is not UV resistant. A Quonset greenhouse can be used for the entire process – from seeding to cultivating mature plants.

d. **Even-Span Greenhouse:** One can build this type of greenhouse as either attached to the main house or as a standalone structure. It has two slopes with equal pitch and width. This type of greenhouse is flexible in design and can provide more space for plants. A standalone even-span greenhouse will require a separate heating system during winter. This greenhouse can be designed as a single span structure or as a multiple span structure.

e. **A-Frame Greenhouse:** This type of greenhouse is relatively simple to construct. As the name indicates, this greenhouse has two walls leaning against each other that resemble the letter 'A'; this greenhouse has to be secured on a foundation and can have same slope or variable slope. One of the main disadvantages is the available floor space – it is small in relation to the height of the structure. This causes problems during winter when the heat rises far above the height of the plants – should you opt for A-frame greenhouse, make arrangements to use fans to blow down the heat towards the plants.

f. **Ridge and Furrow type Greenhouse:** This is typically a A-frame greenhouse where two or more A-frame greenhouses are connected along the length of the eave. The sidewalls are eliminated in this type, thereby giving large floor space; this reduces the cost of maintenance and labor. Due to the lack of sidewalls, heat is well preserved within the greenhouse. The only drawback is that proper care must be taken to dislodge the snow during winter, as the snow cannot slide away on the slopes. Another variation to this type of greenhouse is the **Saw Tooth Greenhouse** where the roof ventilation alone accounts for 25% of the total ventilation of the covered structure.

Based on Utility:

a. **Greenhouses for Active Cooling:** During summer months, it is necessary to make arrangements to draw huge amounts of cool air into the greenhouse. The arrangements/modifications are made using evaporator cooling pads with fan. If you plan to use your greenhouse extensively during summer, design the greenhouse to have at least 40% roof opening.

b. **Greenhouses for Active Heating:** Some might intend to grow crops extensively during winter months and for such purposes one must use heating systems. It is also necessary to construct the greenhouse with thermo pane glasses or double layer polyethylene.

Since the main function here is to retain heat, it is important to calculate the heat lost to the external environment.

Based on Construction Material:

The type of material used for constructing greenhouses majorly depends on the span of the greenhouses. A greenhouse with a large span requires sturdy construction materials. Based on the type of material used, greenhouses can be divided into:

a. **Wooden Framed Structures:** Wood frames are used as structural elements in greenhouses spanning less than 6 meters. Pinewood is the commonly used wood, as it is sturdy, yet cheap. Pinewood is used for erecting the columns and side posts of the greenhouse.

b. **Pipe Framed Structures:** PVC pipes are commonly used as structural elements in a pipe framed greenhouse. This design is adopted when the greenhouse span is around 12 meters. Pipes are used for purlins, cross ties, side posts, and columns. The greenhouses constructed using PVC are low on aesthetic appeal and less durable. However, using UV-resistant pipes can increase the durability.

c. **Truss Framed Structures:** Trusses are used in greenhouse construction when the span is equal to or exceeds 15 meters. Various materials such as tubular steel, flat steel, or angular iron can be used in truss construction. Columns are used only for wide truss framed greenhouses – for width exceeding 21.3 meters. Greenhouses built using glass make use of truss-framed structures.

Based on Covering Materials:

Covering materials used for greenhouses play a major role in retaining and maintaining the heat within the structure. The type frames used for constructing greenhouses depends on the type of covering material. Following are the different types of covering materials that can be used in the construction of greenhouses:

a. **Glass:** Glass conducts sunlight efficiently, and has exceptional clarity; it has a better life than any other material. An insulated glass provides the same insulation value as a double layer, air-inflated poly plastic. The main disadvantage is that glass is expensive, prone to damage during hailstorm, and has the potential to burn the plants as it has high degree of clarity.

b. **Plastic film:** Plastic film is a popular covering material for greenhouses as they are cheap. They can be made of PVC, polyester, or polyethylene and do not cause burning of plants. The main disadvantage is its lifespan – it has to be replaced every 4 years.

c. **Rigid panel:** Rigid panels common in various materials such as acrylic, polycarbonate, fiberglass, and PVC. They are mainly used for Quonset or ridge and furrow type greenhouses. Rigid panels are highly durable – they provide better durability than glass and plastic. However, these panels are prone to collect dust and algae, which reduce the clarity considerably.

Chapter 3

Elements of a Greenhouse

There are many elements to build and manage in a greenhouse, such as foundations, walls, frames, provisions for heating/cooling, plumbing, electricity, etc. The main element to consider before proceeding with your greenhouse construction is to check with your local municipal office about zoning and building permits rules and regulations. It is possible to get fined for constructing a building meant for agricultural purposes in a residential zone. Once you have worked through the zoning rules, it is time for you to lay the foundation for your greenhouse.

Foundations:

Following are the steps to follow before laying the foundation:

1. Select a level surface – to do this you have to use/buy a **level**, which consists of a glass tube containing a liquid with a trapped air bubble. When a surface is level, the air bubble will remain in the center of the tube.

    a. Mark the four corners where the greenhouse walls are to be erected.

    b. At each corner place a 2x4 – keep the **level** to check if the surface is level.

    c. Adjust the side that is not level either by adding or removing soil.

2. Check the selected site for sunlight exposure – it is preferable to do this in summer and on a sunny day.

    a. If the selected site receives sunlight for 6 hours or more than that, it is the perfect site for your greenhouse.

    b. If the site receives sunlight for 4 to 6 hours, it is partly sunny – you may have to supplement your greenhouse with additional lighting.

    c. If the site receives sunlight for less than 4 hours, it is partly shaded – you have to reconsider the site for your greenhouse.

    d. If there is no sunlight at all, the site is completely shaded and definitely not the correct location for your greenhouse.

3. Mark the dimensions for the greenhouse on the selected site. Use 2ft high 2x2 stakes to mark the corners; measure the diagonals – they must be equal; string lines from stake to stake.

4. If you are planning for a concrete foundation, use batter boards at each corner to ensure a level surface.

    a. Batter boards are horizontal boards that are attached to the corners of your site to show the exact layout of the foundation.

    b. You will need three 2x4 stakes for each corner.

    c. At each corner: measure out 2ft from the corner in line with the diagonal and drive a stake (let us call this *Stake A*).

    d. From *Stake A* measure out 4ft in both directions (parallel to the perimeter); the three stakes must form a right angle.

    e. Nail 1x4 boards at the top of the stakes to connect them.

    f. String another set of lines above the original lines (refer step: 3).

    g. Cut small lines in the batter boards corresponding to the original lines.

    h. Attach the new set of strings (step: f) within the cuts – use a line level or water level to mark an equal elevation.

    i. Remove the original stakes and strings.

Concrete Foundation:

For constructing a concrete foundation, you must first dig a trench, pour the footing and build up the walls of the foundation. If you live in an area that is subjected to harsh winter or if the soil is loose, you will need a concrete foundation to support your greenhouse. Before pouring the concrete footings, check with your local building inspector to determine the frost line – the footing must start from below the frost line. The footing width is usually twice the width of the wall. If you need a heavier foundation, you must first pour the concrete footing and then build up the wall using concrete blocks.

If the soil is loose or sandy, you must forms to hold the concrete as it is poured. Lay 2 pieces of reinforcing horizontal bars (rebar) in the trench – 2 to 3 inches from the bottom; you can use bricks to support the bars from the bottom. For the forms, brace ½ inch plywood using 2x4 lumber. Once the forms are set in place, pour the concrete and allow it to set. Once the concrete is hardened, you can either pour a concrete wall or build a wall from concrete blocks.

Concrete Slab Foundation:

A 3" thick concrete slab foundation is usually used for home greenhouses. If you are building an attached greenhouse, the finished floor of the greenhouse must be a couple of steps below the house floor. However, for a freestanding greenhouse, the finished floor must be several inches above the outside finish grade. The floor thickness of the greenhouse must be 3" and the outside edges must be thicker to withstand the weight and cracking from frost. It is important to add 4" of compacted gravel for drainage purposes. On top of the gravel, add a layer of 6 mil polyethylene to act as a moisture barrier.

Wood Foundation:

Wood foundation is simple to build and also inexpensive – it is the popular choice of foundation for greenhouse construction. It is recommended to use decay resistant woods such as cedar, cypress, or redwood. Following are the steps for building a wooden foundation:

1. Level the site and mark the perimeter.

2. Dig a trench on the perimeter – this must be 6 inches below grade; it must also be a couple of inches wider than the lumber (usually 4x4 lumber is used).

3. Fill 2 inches of the trench with gravel.

4. Stack the lumber on top of one another and fasten them using large galvanized deck screws.

5. To secure the frame to the ground, drive L-shaped rebars through the frame into the ground.

Plumbing and Wiring:

It is always recommended to use a licensed plumber and electrician to carry out the plumbing and wiring of your greenhouse. Should you decide to carry out these works, please exercise caution; also check with your local authorities about the nature of works that you can carry out without hiring professionals. Some building code regulations expect you to hire a utilities company and/or licensed electrician for certain aspects of works to be completed.

Following are some pointers to help you with your plumbing and wiring:

1. If you are building an attached greenhouse, it is easier to run a house from the outdoor tap; you can run a hose if the greenhouse is nearby to the house.

2. An outside tap might not be feasible during winter, in which case you must install a permanent waterline – you must install a water pipeline below the frost line with a back-flow prevention valve before laying the foundation; lack of back-flow valve might contaminate your main water line.

3. If you are undecided about the type of irrigation and electrical equipment to be used in the greenhouse, install a 4" or 6" pipe through the footing before pouring the foundation; this pipe can be used to install the utilities later on.

4. It is preferable to use a 22mm pipe that is connected to a dry hydrant inside the greenhouse.

5. Consider installing an automated drip irrigation system that can water the plants twice a day.

6. Make arrangements for a misting system – it will help in maintaining the temperature and regulating the humidity in the greenhouse.

7. Provide water outlets at regular intervals in the greenhouse for proper draining of water.

8. Usually a slope (in the ground) of 1/8 or ¼ per foot is provided to drain the water – this is done before setting up the foundation and the slope acts as the outside drainage for your greenhouse.

9. It is necessary to provide drainage within the greenhouse too – you can install drains and make your greenhouse floor slope towards the drains. Thus, it is important to sketch out the drainage requirements before you start constructing the greenhouse.

10. If you have a large greenhouse, check with your local authorities about regulations regarding draining of pesticides and fertilizers.

11. Hire an electrician to check if your house has the capacity to supply electricity for the greenhouse too.

12. A small greenhouse needs 120v to operate the fan, vents, and lights; if you are building a large greenhouse, or using electricity to generate heat you will need 240v to meet the electrical demands.

13. Use a plastic conduit to install the wiring in the greenhouse.

14. Use a ground fault circuit interrupter and only outdoor rated UF cable.

15. If you are planning to use gas or propane to heat your greenhouse, a certified technician must install the gas supply line piping.

Flooring:

Many people might consider it a waste of money to build a greenhouse floor. However, lack of flooring material will leave the entire greenhouse muddy, thereby inviting weeds, insects, diseases, and pests. If you do not want to spend money on the flooring, try using gravel – it is a low cost option, which also helps in efficient drainage of water. The gravel or any equivalent loose material must be laid several inches thick on a weed barrier – the barrier must not be made of plastic. This will not only improve the drainage but also the humidity and heat.

If you are interested in creating a permanent flooring/pathway, use bricks or stones and set them in mortar.

Advantages of permanent floor:

- Once installed, the floor will remain in a good condition for years to come.
- You can fix the sinks, benches, cabinets, and other accessories on the floor.
- A permanent floor requires minimum maintenance – cleaning whenever it is dirty – similar to your house floor.

Advantages of temporary floor:

- Cost of laying a temporary floor that is made of gravel or bricks is economical.
- You can make space on the floor to grow additional plants.
- Changing the floor is easy – all you need is a shovel to remove the gravel/brick.

Framing:

The frames for your greenhouse can be constructed using various materials such as wood, aluminum, PVC, and steel; it is also possible to build frames using masonry. However, each material has its distinct advantages and disadvantages as mentioned below:

Wood:

Wood framing is attractive, doesn't transfer heat and has minimum condensation issues. Naturally rot-resistant wood such as redwood and cedar can be used for longevity. On the flip side, it is bulky, can cast shadows on plants and requires regular maintenance.

Aluminum:

Aluminum frame is easy to maintain, can be anodized and power-coated, can be used with various glazing systems, is durable and long lasting. Disadvantages are that aluminum loses heat quickly, has condensation problems, and cheap quality aluminum cannot withstand heavy winds and snowfall.

Poly Vinyl Chloride:

Also known as PVC, it is an inexpensive material suitable for beginners. It is lightweight and therefore is portable. The main disadvantage is that it cannot withstand high winds or snowfall and the glazing material is restricted to plastic sheets.

Framing of Walls and Roof:

If you are already familiar with framing, it will be an easy task to frame your greenhouse. However, if you are new to framing, you must accustom yourself with framing terminologies, and how to use a framing square. Frames are usually assembled separately and then attached to the house. It is important to construct a frame on a level surface. Some of the terms commonly used in framing are:

1. Rafters – these are sloping beams that support the roof sheathing.

2. Stud – a vertical member used in framing walls; it usually comes in standard sizes such as 2"x4", 2"x3", or 2"x6".

3. Plates – 2"x4" horizontal supports used for attaching studs at top and bottom.

4. Ledger board – a 2x6 lumber attached to the studs along an existing wall; usually lag screws are used.

5. Framing square – also called 'Carpenter's square', it is a L-shaped tool used to mark right angles; one side of the square is the same width as a 2x4.

6. Lumber comes in standard lengths: 8, 10, 12, 14, and 16 feet.

Wall Framing Tips:

1. Cut the rafters, studs, and plates based on the dimensions of your greenhouse.

2. Before cutting the studs, consider the allowance required for top and bottom plates.

3. A stud must be placed at every 2ft on the center.

4. Exercise caution while cutting plates for end walls – the width of a 2x4 lumber is 3.5"; if you have a 7ft wall, the plates will be 6'5" long.

5. To frame the wall: place the top and bottom plates side by side on a level surface.

6. Using a framing square mark 2ft apart on both plates simultaneously.

7. Arrange the studs on the marking and nail together the plates and studs.

8. Once you raise the frame, use a level to constantly check for proper vertical and horizontal alignment of the frame.

Framing of Doors and Vents:

Before you start with the framing work for your greenhouse, it is necessary to plan the vent positions. Most greenhouses have louvers and doors in the front and back walls; vents are added usually along the ridge and the sides.

1. When framing an allowance of ¼" must be provided to accommodate the width of doors and vents.

2. It might become necessary to rearrange the studs – if you can't achieve 2' o.c. with the studs, move them farther apart or bring them closer, but do not eliminate studs.

3. Use a 2x4 header on top of the door opening; this usually runs the width of the wall.

4. Add braces between the door and adjacent studs to provide stability.

5. Cross circulation of air can be achieved through placing vents on the opposite sides; you can opt for either manual or automatic vents.

6. The square footage of vent required for the greenhouse = 0.2xsquare footage of the floor.

7. If you live in a hot climate consider placing roof vents; as hot air rises through the roof vents, the temperature in the greenhouse will go down.

Roof Framing:

Following are some pointers for framing your roof:

1. Use 2x4 rafters at 2ft on center; these rafters must line up with the wall studs.

2. If you live in an area with heavy snowfall and/or have a large span greenhouse, use 2x6 lumber instead of 2x4.

3. Use nails to attach the rafters to the top plate and ridge board.

4. Do not cut all the rafters at once; measure the rafter dimensions, cut a couple of rafters, and check for proper fit.

5. Nail braces between the rafters to strengthen the roof; you can cut short pieces from 2x4 to use as braces.

Heating:

Keeping your greenhouse warm during cold weather is extremely important. You can generate heat using either gas or electric heaters. If you are using propane, oil, or kerosene heaters, make sure the greenhouse is adequately vented. You can also consider heating using hot water; here, hot water circulates through pipes set around the perimeter of your greenhouse under the benches.

Calculating Heat Requirements for your Greenhouse:

The heat output (expressed in Btu – British Thermal Units) required for your greenhouse can be calculated using the following formula:

Btu = Area x Difference x 1.1

    Area = total square footage of your greenhouse panels

    Difference = (coldest night temperature in your locality – minimum night temperature required by your plants)

    1.1 = average heat loss factor of glazing

For a greenhouse that uses double glazed glass or twin-wall polycarbonate, the Btu can be reduced by 30%; a 50% reduction in Btu is possible for greenhouses that use triple glazing.

Heat Conservation Tips:

- You can save energy by keeping the greenhouse cool at night – maintain a temperature of 50^0F.

- You can make a small heated chamber within your greenhouse to place pots containing germination seeds and seedlings

- Also, keep the glazing clean – a dirty surface allows less light inside

- Using a storm door will help prevent drafts

- Insulate all heating supply lines

- If you have an attached greenhouse, redirect the heat exhausted by the dryer into your greenhouse

- Install an alarm system to alert you about power failure or temperature changes in the greenhouse
-

Cooling:

While it is important to maintain heat in your greenhouse for optimal plant growth, excess heat will damage the plants and the produce. Thus, it is equally important to have cooling systems to manage and maintain optimal temperatures within your greenhouse. Apart from providing vents to cool the greenhouse, use of shading materials, evaporative cooling and fans are also effective.

One of the best ways to keep the greenhouse cool is to reduce the heat. This can be done effectively by manipulating the amount of sunlight entering the greenhouse. You can use shade cloths, blinds, or spray-on shades.

Shade cloth:

This is a woven or knitted cloth made from polyester, polyethylene, or polypropylene. It prevents the damage caused to plants due to direct sunlight exposure but doesn't reduce the heat inside the greenhouse. The advantage of shade cloth is that it is lightweight and offers different degrees of shade ranging from 5% to 95%. You can start using shade cloth from late spring; precaution must be taken to leave the roof vents open.

Blinds:

Retractable blinds are available in wood and aluminum. The advantage of blinds is that the amount of sunlight can be adjusted based on the greenhouse requirements and weather conditions.

Shading compound:

A shading compound contains ground pigments that reflect sunlight. It is used to control the entry of heat and is applied to the glazing of the greenhouse. The compound must be diluted with water before applying. Some types of compounds can be easily removed whereas others are meant for permanent application.

Evaporative Cooling:

It is possible to achieve an inside temperature, which is 20^0F lesser than the outside greenhouse temperature using Evaporating cooling. The simplest way to achieve evaporative cooling is to hose down the greenhouse floor. However, since evaporation from the floor is slow, it has to be hosed down frequently, making it ineffective.

A swamp cooler is efficient in providing evaporative cooling; it consists of a blower and a cellulose pad with a water pump, and is mounted on a concrete pad next to the greenhouse. The dry outside air that is drawn through the swamp cooler is moistened through the wet pads and is blown into the greenhouse. This moist air in turn picks up the heat within the greenhouse and is released outside through the vents.

Greenhouse Maintenance:

Your greenhouse requires regular maintenance and a slight complacence on your part can lead to inflections, decay, and/or wilting of plants. Greenhouse maintenance falls into two categories:

1. Daily maintenance
2. Seasonal maintenance

Maintenance Checklist:

- ✓ Check the leaves (especially the underneath) for pests; remove decayed leaves.
- ✓ Collect all the withered leaves and discard them; keep the floor clean of debris and dirt.
- ✓ Stack fertilizers, soil, and other tools in a clean and dry place.

- ✓ Check for leaks, rust, and other damages in the supply line, if not every day, at least weekly.
- ✓ Clean the glazing, as a dirty glazing will reduce the amount of sunlight entering the greenhouse.
- ✓ Clean and oil all the fans, vents, and louvers; clean gutters and screens on a weekly basis.
- ✓ Remove any damaged and/or decayed wood without delay as it can lead to fungal growth.
- ✓ During spring/summer – apply shades/blinds/shading compound.
- ✓ During autumn/winter – remove the shades/blinds/shading compound.

Apart from the regular maintenance it is necessary to carry out an annual maintenance of your greenhouse. You can do this in autumn:

1. Remove all the plants from your greenhouse and place it outside.

2. Turn off the power supply to the greenhouse.

3. Use a bleach to scrub the inside of the greenhouse including walls, benches, frames, doors, windows, and floors.

4. Allow the inside to dry completely; before moving the plants inside check for pests and decay.

5. Now clean the outside using water or special solutions meant for glazed windows and doors.

Chapter 4

Greenhouse Plans

Download High Resolution Greenhouse plans from our website **HERE**

http://sdsplans.com

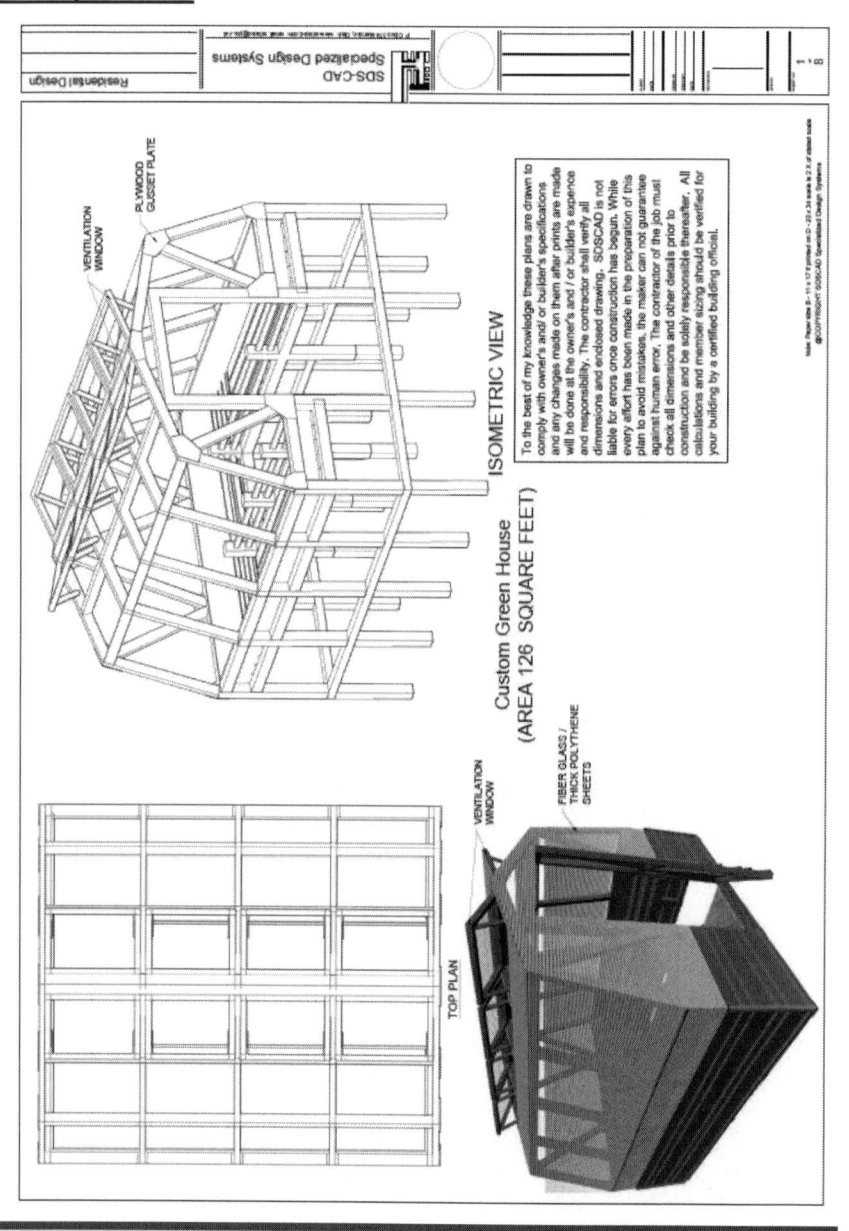

How to Build a Greenhouse

How to Build a Greenhouse

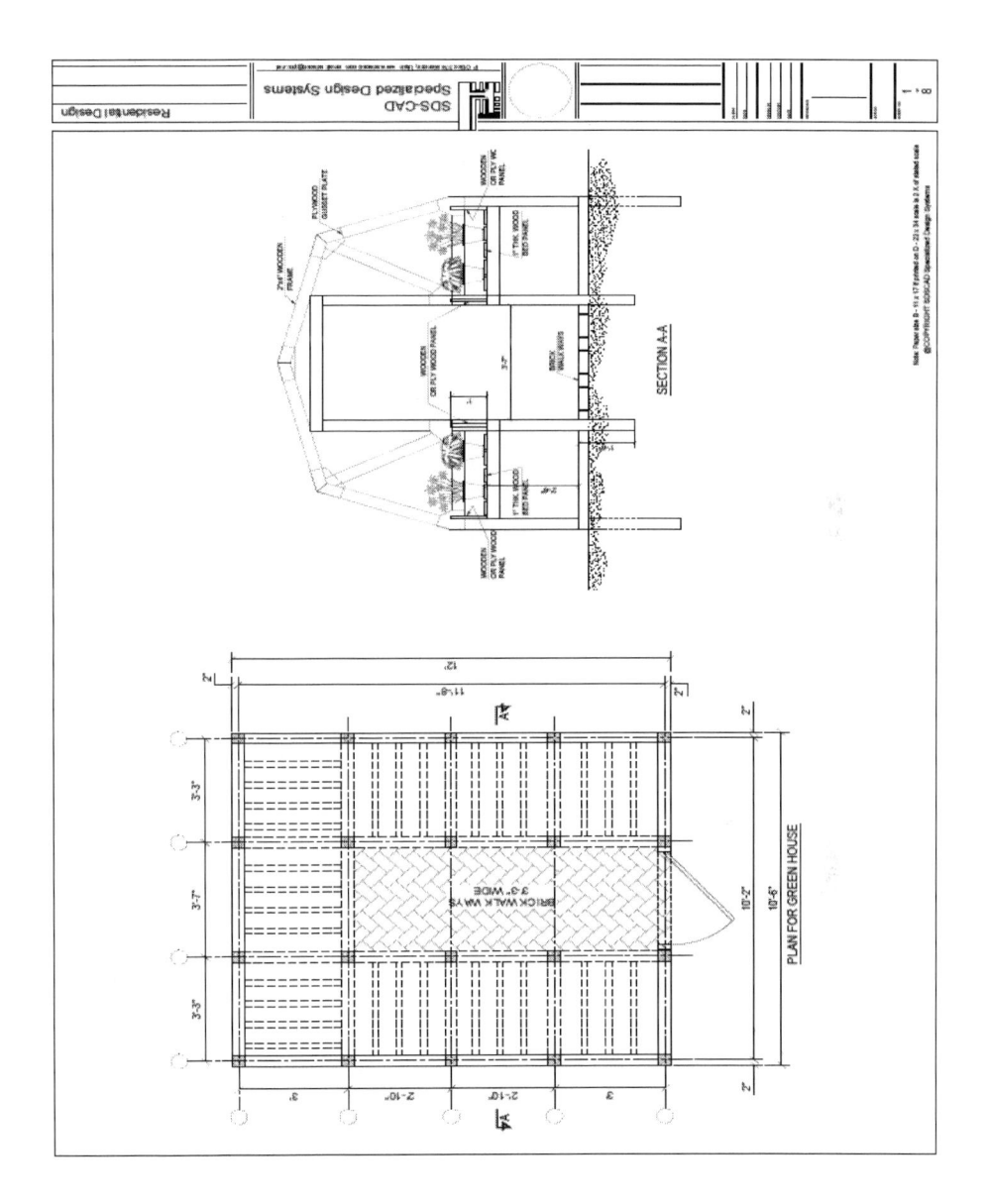

How to Build a Greenhouse

Page 32

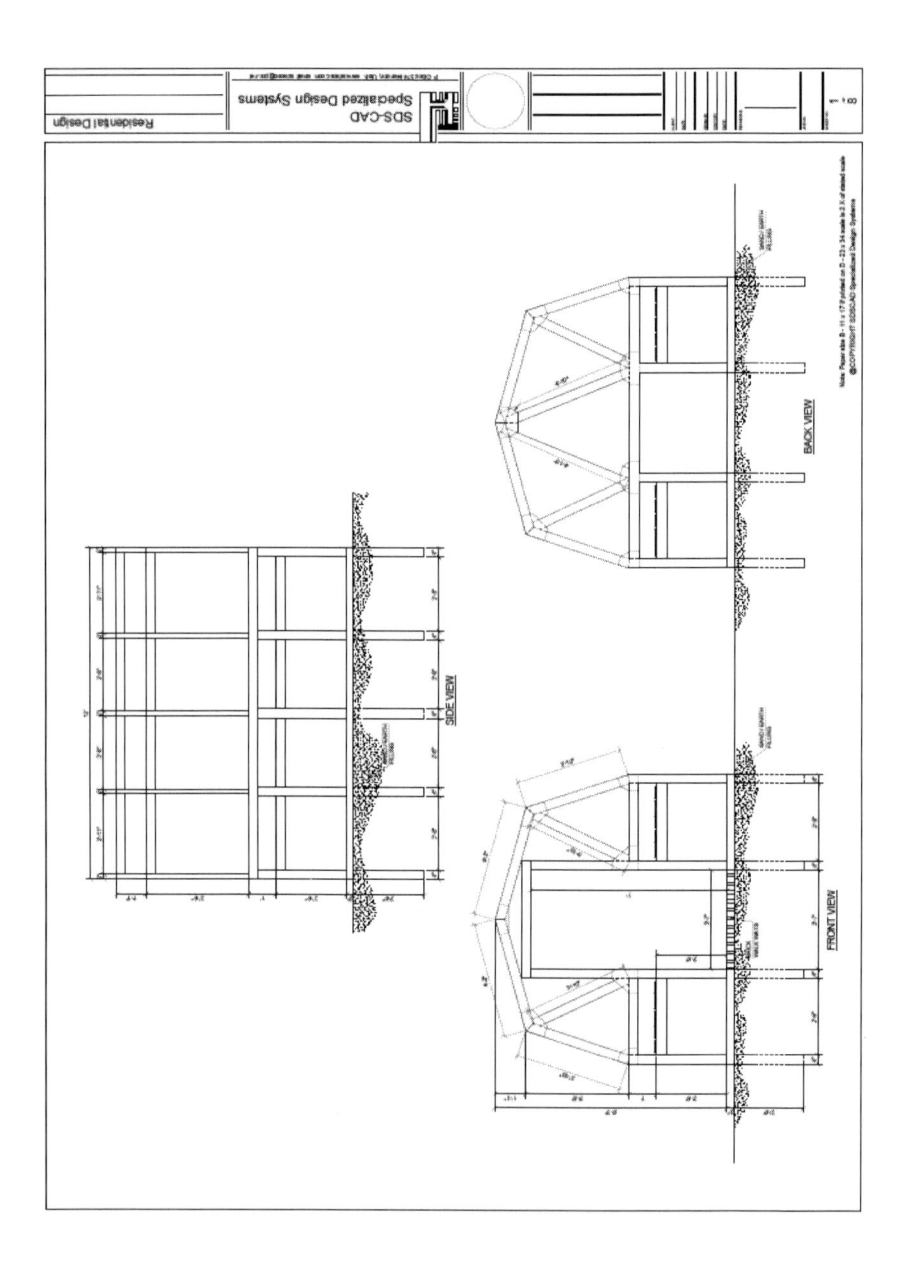

Step by step plans to build a barn style Greenhouse

Introduction:

This greenhouse is 10ft wide by 14ft and stands 10' off the ground at the highest point.

Description:

You should set the location of the small greenhouse in such a manner that it gets maximum sunlight all day long. If you have a large garden, the best solution is to place it far away from buildings or trees, otherwise try to build it as to get the morning light from east. This aspect is essential for your project, therefore pay attention when choosing the location of your greenhouse. Your hard work will pay off on the long run, as plants need the sunlight to produce food, especially in the morning.

Choosing the right materials for the job might be a difficult task at first, as you need time to decide the best solution to your own needs. If you have a small budget and want to get the job done quickly, we recommend you to build a wooden greenhouse, using

undertake a serious project or you prefer a light construction, you should consider using PVC pipes. Nevertheless, in this article we show you plans for a small wooden greenhouse, to help you grow your own organic vegetables and keep the plants in an appropriate climate during the winters.

How to Build a Greenhouse

Step 1. The Greenouse base :

Use 4" x 4" (100 mm x 100 mm) treated, or natural decay-resistant, sawn wood to make the base.
Make a rectangle 10ft" x 14ft" as shown in the drawing above. Fix the wood together in the corners by using galvanized nails and nail plates.
Before you site (position) the base, make sure the ground where the base will rest is level and firm.
Use a level or a water level to check the grade, and dig accordingly to level the ground directly beneath where the wood will be sitting.
Check that the two diagonal measurements are equal. If they are not, make any necessary adjustments. When the diagonals are equal, then the base is square.
Secure the base in place by driving stakes into the ground around the perimeter.
Nail the stakes to the base and cut flush any stakes protruding higher than the base wood.

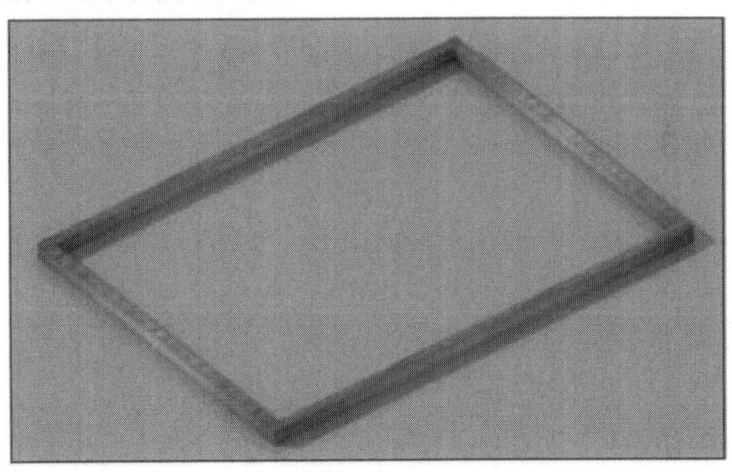

Step 2. The side wall-frames :

Construct all the framing out of 1 1/2" x 3 1/2" (90 mm x 45 mm) treated, or natural decay-resistant wood.
On a flat surface, make up the two side wall frames to the dimensions shown in the above drawing.
Make the diagonal measurements equal, and when the frame is square, cut and fix the bracing members in place.

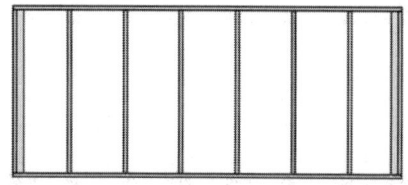

Step 3. The roof frame sections :

Make up five roof sections that span from side-wall to side-wall. Refer to the plans and instructions below.
Cut all roof frame pieces to the dimensions given above.
Use 1 1/2" x 3 1/2" (90 mm x 45 mm) treated, or natural decay-resistant wood.
In all, cut 5 long rafters, 5 short rafters and 5 rafter uprights all with end angle cuts as shown in the plan drawing.
Also cut five triangular gussets (equilateral triangles) from a sheet of 3/8" (10mm) treated plywood, with all three sides being 20" (500 mm) long.
On a flat piece of ground, make up the five roof sections to the pattern and dimensions as shown in above drawing. Ensure the two furthest points are 10ft" apart and then nail the triangular gussets in place with galvanized flathead nails spaced every 2" (50 mm) apart, one gusset to each roof section.

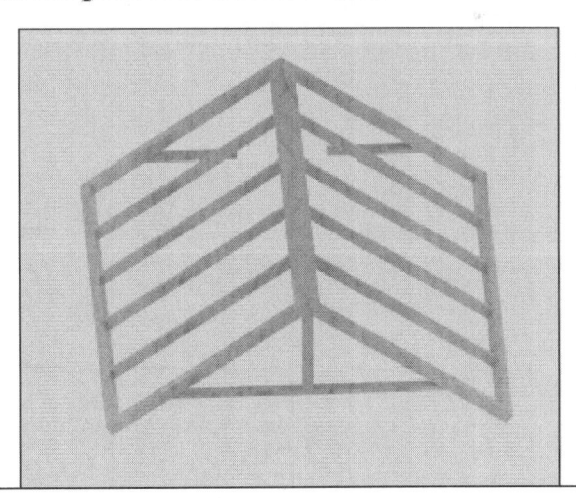

Step 4. Side walls and roof sections :

Stand the two side walls upright on the base boards and support them with temporarily props. Fix the bottom plate of the side walls to the base with galvanized nails.
Lift the 5 roof sections in place on top of the side walls.
First position a roof section at each end of the side walls, and then position the other three evenly spaced in between.
Fix the roof frames to the side wall top plate with galvanized nails

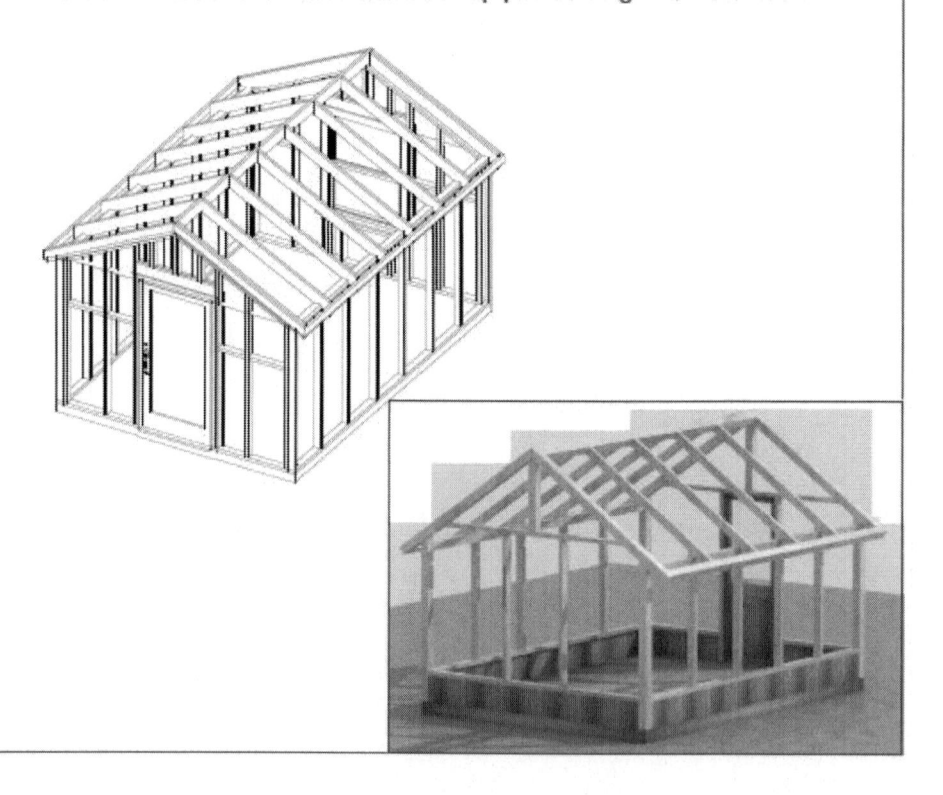

Step 5. The doors :

Make the doors as per the dimensions given in the drawing - the front door.
Make the doors 3/4" (20 mm) smaller than the opening.
Use 1 1/2" x 1 1/2" (45 mm x 45 mm) stock for the stiles (upright side pieces), and use 1 1/2" x 3 1/2" (90 mm x 45 mm) stock for the three horizontal rails.
Make the door frames up on a flat surface. Ensure the frames are square and then nail the gussets in place on both sides of the doors.
Hinge the doors in place and fit handles or padbolts of your choice.

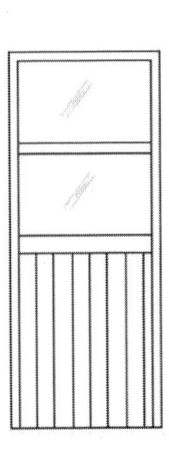

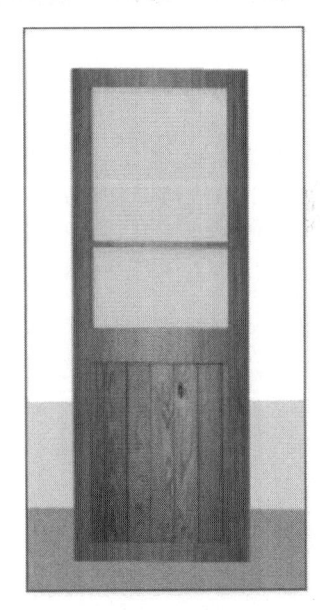

How to Build a Greenhouse

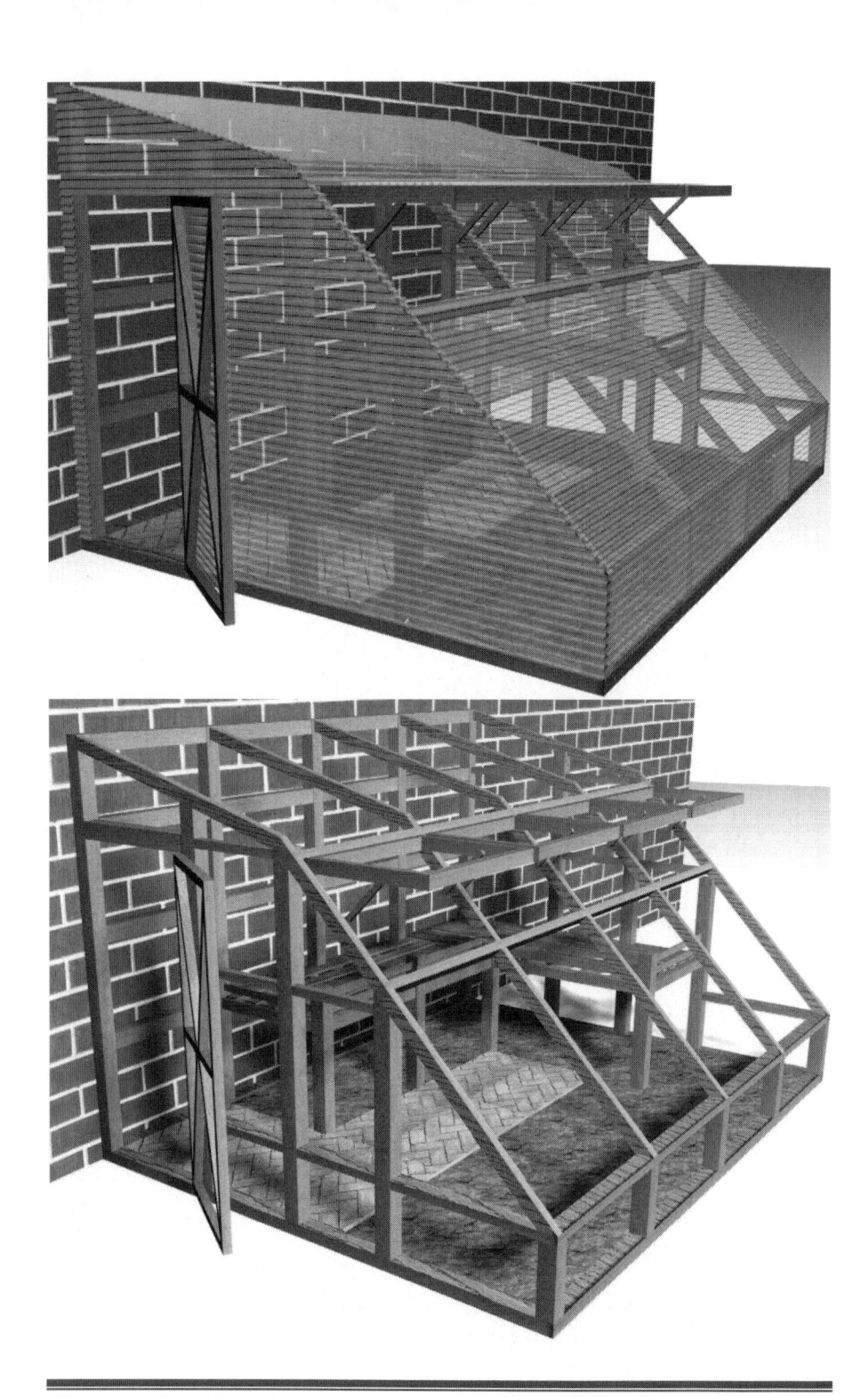

How to Build a Greenhouse

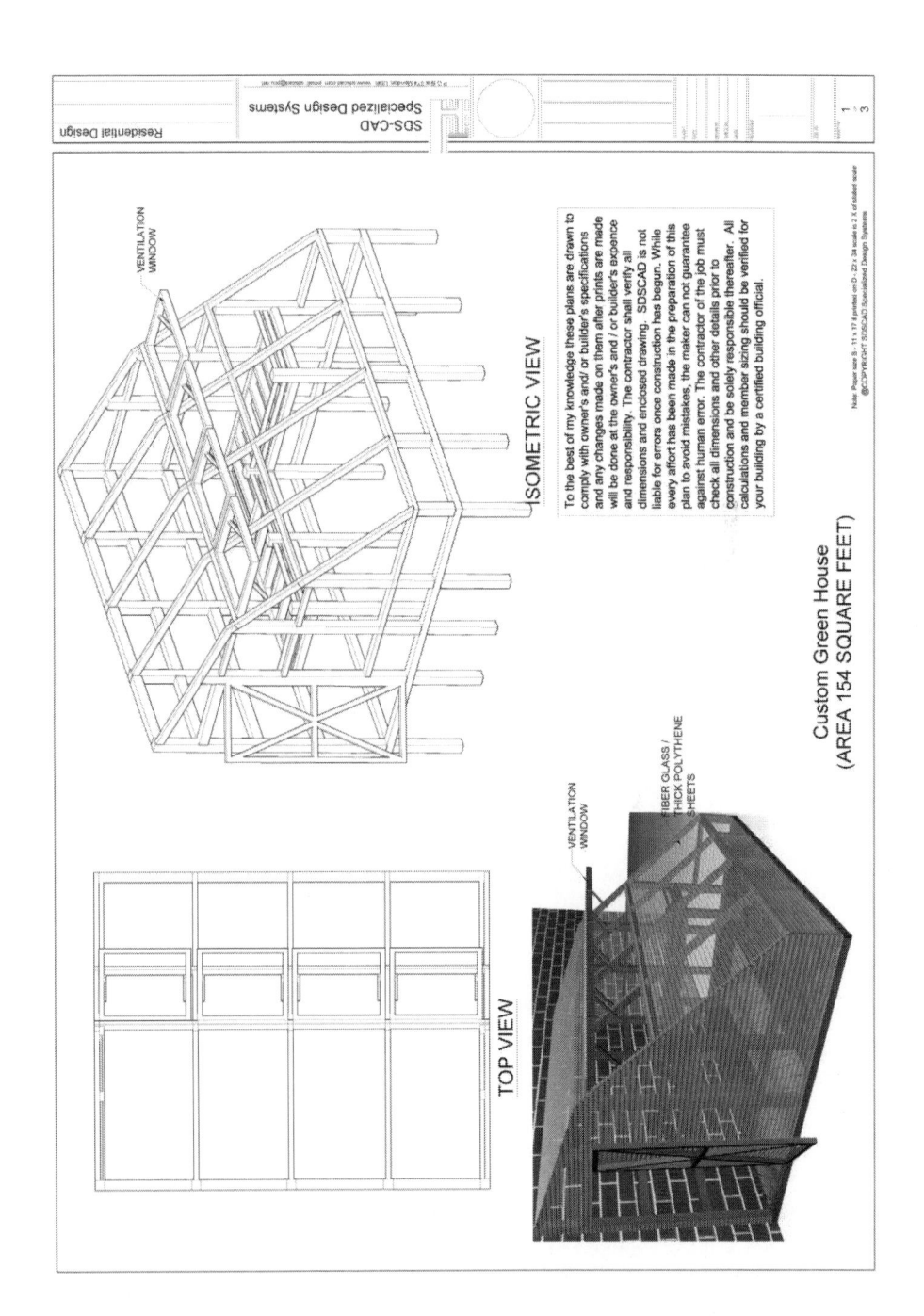

Page 41

How to Build a Greenhouse

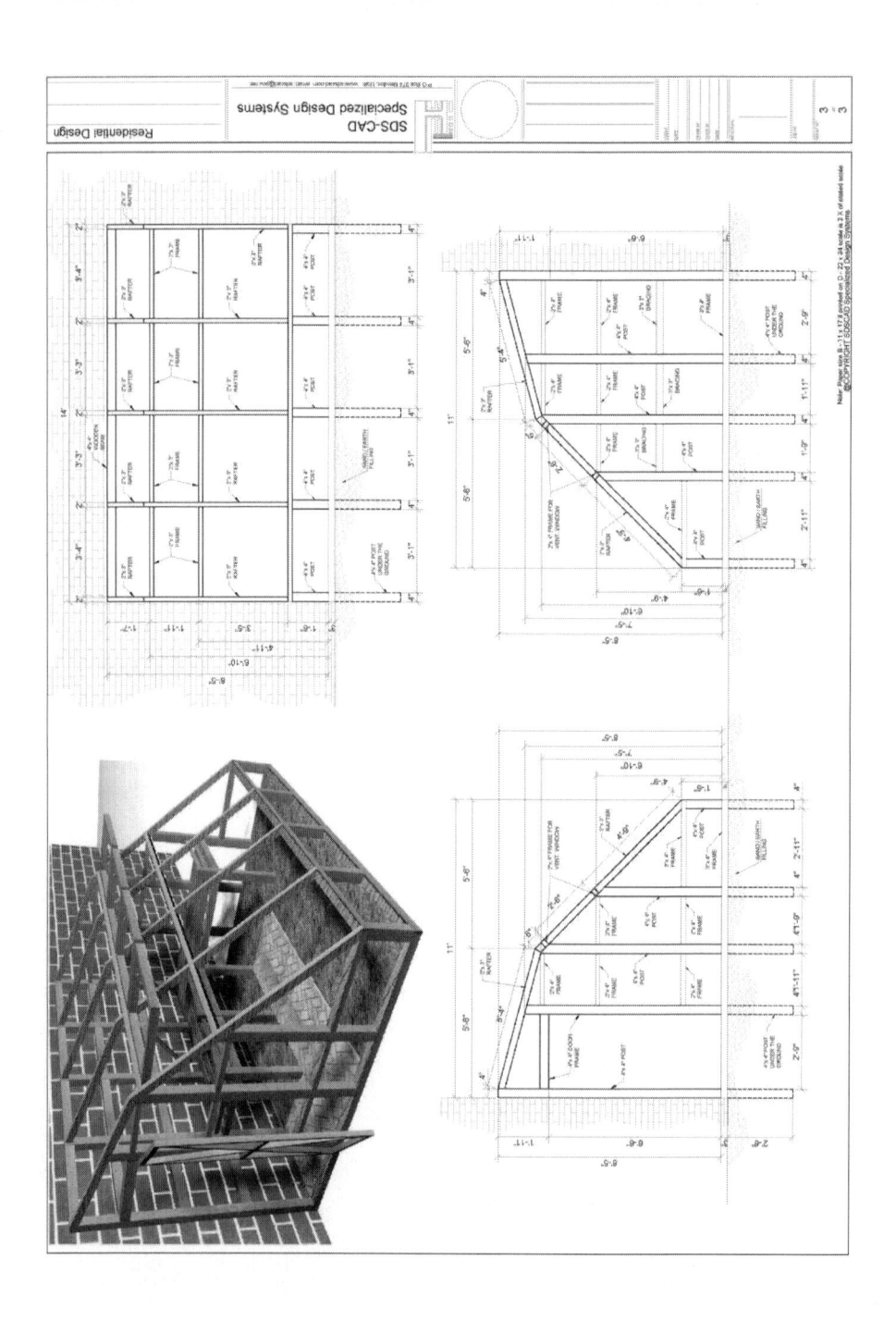

Page 42

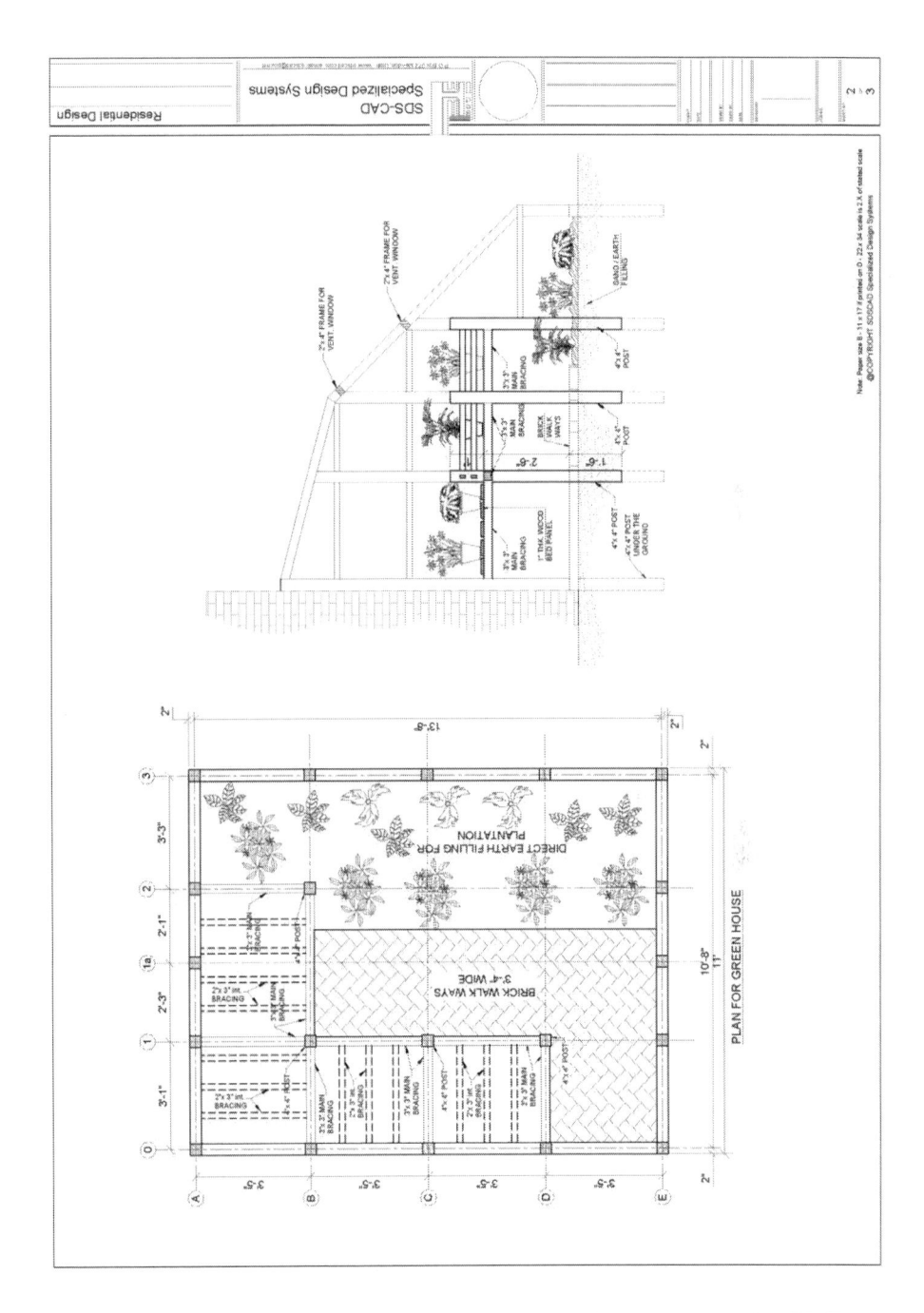

Download High Resolution Greenhouse plans from our website **HERE**

Http://sdsplans.com

How to Build a Greenhouse

How to Build a Greenhouse

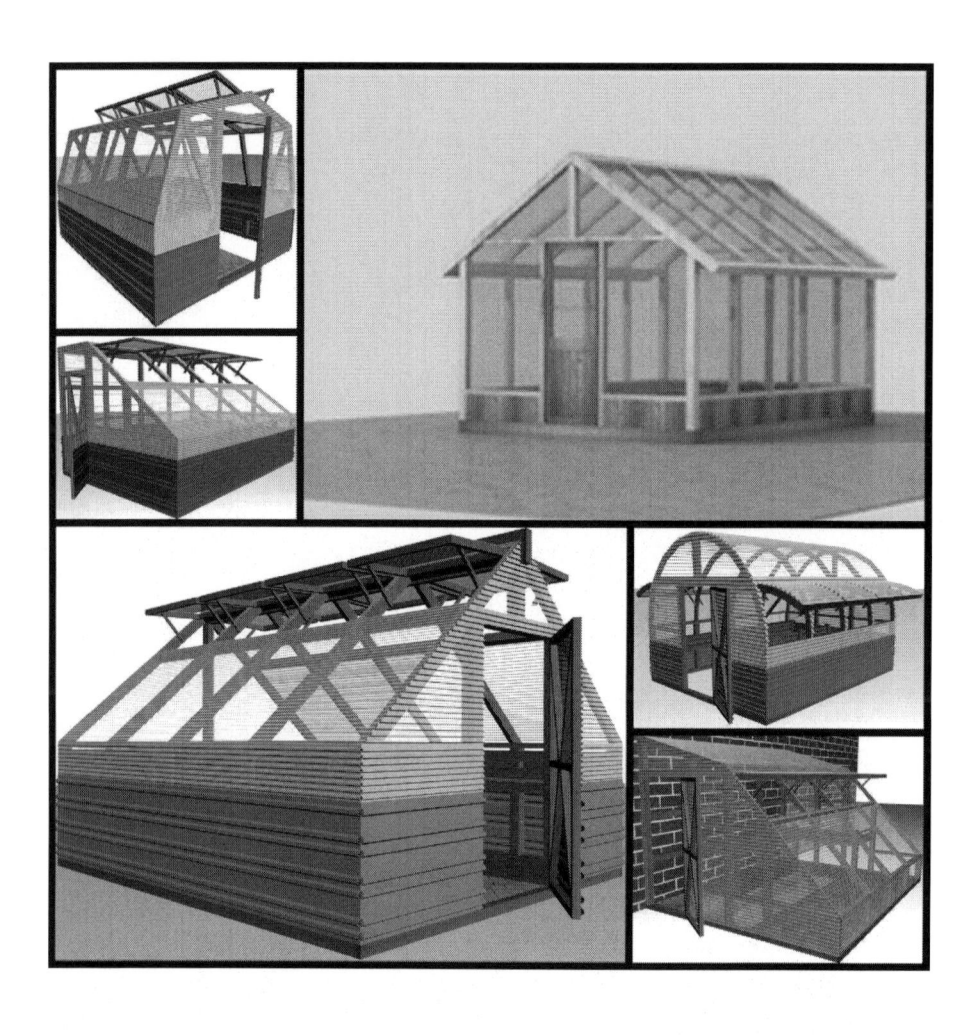

Page 44

Check out some of the other JD-Biz Publishing books

Gardening Series on Amazon

Download Free Books!

http://MendonCottageBooks.com

How to Build a Greenhouse

Health Learning Series

Country Life Books

GRANDMA'S
NATURAL REMEDIES AND ANCIENT HERBAL BEAUTY RECIPES
Volume 1
HEALTH LEARNING SERIES
DUEEP J SINGH AND J DAVIDSON
GRANDMA'S
NATURAL REMEDIES AND ANCIENT HERBAL BEAUTY RECIPES
Volume 2
HEALTH LEARNING SERIES
DUEEP J SINGH AND J DAVIDSON
GRANDMA'S
NATURAL REMEDIES AND ANCIENT RECIPES
GRANDMA'S CURE FOR OBESITY
GRANDMA'S CURE FOR THE COMMON COLD
Volume 3
HEALTH LEARNING SERIES
DUEEP J SINGH AND J DAVIDSON
GRANDMA'S
NATURAL REMEDIES AND ANCIENT HERBAL RECIPES
Volume 4
HEALTH LEARNING SERIES
DUEEP J SINGH AND J DAVIDSON
GRANDMA'S
HERBAL LORE
ANCIENT HERBAL RECIPES AND REMEDIES
Volume 5
HEALTH LEARNING SERIES
DUEEP J SINGH AND J DAVIDSON
GRANDMA'S
ANCIENT BEAUTY REMEDIES FROM HER KITCHEN
Volume 6
HEALTH LEARNING SERIES
DUEEP J SINGH AND J DAVIDSON
GRANDMA'S
EASY TO USE TIPS IN THE KITCHEN AND OUTDOORS
Volume 7
HEALTH LEARNING SERIES
DUEEP J SINGH AND J DAVIDSON
GRANDMA'S
HOUSEHOLD HINTS AND RECIPES USING TIME TESTED ECONOMICAL TIPS IN YOUR HOME
75 Tips
Remove Stains
Peel Tomatoes
Perfect Pies
HEALTH LEARNING SERIES
DUEEP J SINGH AND J DAVIDSON
GRANDMA'S
NATURAL REMEDIES AND ANCIENT RECIPES
ALL 5 BOOKS IN 1
HEALTH LEARNING SERIES
DUEEP J SINGH AND J DAVIDSON

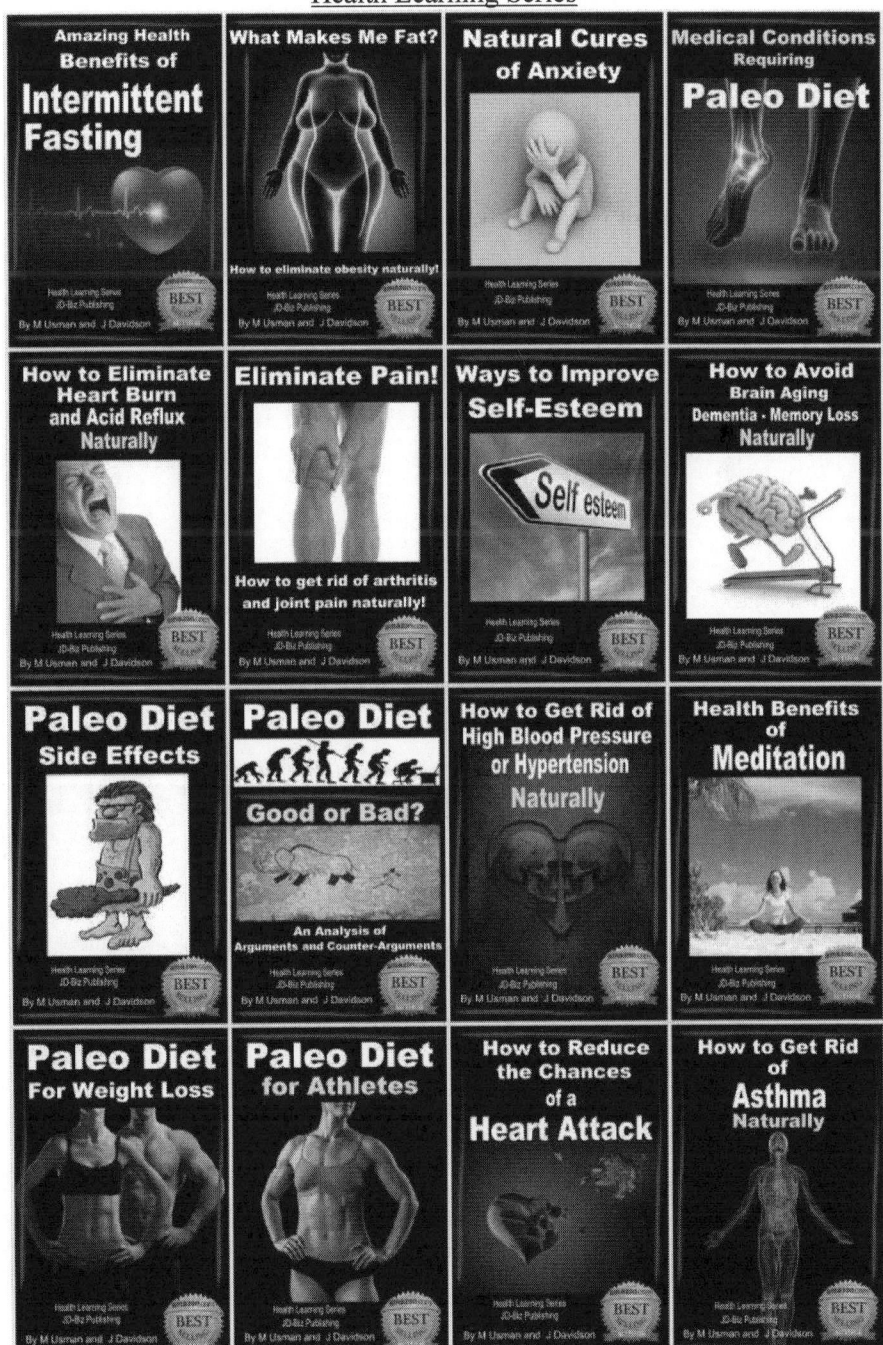

Health Learning Series

- Amazing Health Benefits of Intermittent Fasting
- What Makes Me Fat? How to eliminate obesity naturally!
- Natural Cures of Anxiety
- Medical Conditions Requiring Paleo Diet
- How to Eliminate Heart Burn and Acid Reflux Naturally
- Eliminate Pain! How to get rid of arthritis and joint pain naturally!
- Ways to Improve Self-Esteem
- How to Avoid Brain Aging Dementia - Memory Loss Naturally
- Paleo Diet Side Effects
- Paleo Diet Good or Bad? An Analysis of Arguments and Counter-Arguments
- How to Get Rid of High Blood Pressure or Hypertension Naturally
- Health Benefits of Meditation
- Paleo Diet For Weight Loss
- Paleo Diet for Athletes
- How to Reduce the Chances of a Heart Attack
- How to Get Rid of Asthma Naturally

All titles: Health Learning Series, JD-Biz Publishing, By M Usman and J Davidson

How to Build a Greenhouse — Page 49

Amazing Animal Book Series

Learn To Draw Series

How to Build and Plan Books

Entrepreneur Book Series

Our books are available at

1. Amazon.com
2. Barnes and Noble
3. Itunes
4. Kobo
5. Smashwords
6. Google Play Books

Download Free Books!

http://MendonCottageBooks.com

Publisher

JD-Biz Corp

P O Box 374

Mendon, Utah 84325

http://www.jd-biz.com/

Printed in Great Britain
by Amazon